The Art of Painting

Nature is perfect, but in art man does not need perfect nature... precisely because it is perfect. He needs on the contrary to represent what is inward. The natural appearance must be transformed to obtain a purer vision of nature.

De natuur is volmaakt, maar de mensch heeft geen behoefte aan volmaakte natuur in kunst ... juist omdat de natuur zoo volmaakt is. Hij heeft wel behoefte aan representatie van het meer innerlijke. Men moet de natuurlijke verschijning veranderen, om de natuur meer zuiver te doen zien.

—Piet Mondriaan, August 1919

The Art of Painting

Robert Perry

DUTCH POET PRESS

2024

Copyright © 2024 Robert Perry
Dutch Poet Press
All Rights Reserved.

◆ ◆ ◆

ISBN 978-17342742-4-0

DUTCH POET PRESS

dutchpoetpress.com
rhperry51@gmail.com

Cover Art: Detail of *The Art of Painting*, 1666, oil on canvas, by Jan Vermeer, Kunsthistorische Museum in Vienna, Austria, available in the public domain. Detail of clouds from *View of Haarlem with Bleaching Ground*, c1665, by Jacob van Ruisdael, reprinted with permission from the Mauritshuis, The Hague, The Netherlands.

With love
to Jessie

CONTENTS

1
Sheets of Linen

3   Sheets of Linen
5   van der Helstlaan 16
6   *Clamdigger*
8   Yeck, Doe, Seh, Chahar, Panj
11 Pale Trees of January
12 *Return of the Prodigal Son*
15 Law Giver
16 Vanitas: Memento Mori
18 Vanitas: Unseen Stories
19 Luchtfietser (Daydreamer)
21 After So Many Years

2
If You Asked Me

25 If You Asked Me
27 *River Pavilion, Mountain Colors*
28 Moss Cove, Point Lobos
30 Hawk Hill
31 Great Blue Heron Takes Flight
32 Valley of the Gaping Mouth
34 Early Spring
35 Summer Interior
36 Clarity of Autumn
37 *If Not, Winter*

3
Dance of Hours

- 41 Dance of Hours
- 42 *Perhaps in Spring*
- 43 Before the Revolution
- 44 Barefoot Boy
- 45 Good Government
- 46 Place of Peace (Shiloh)
- 47 Messenger of Love
- 48 The Dead at Antietum
- 50 Soldier in the Night
- 51 Copper and Wood
- 52 Summer Quartet: Morning
- 53 Summer Quartet: Afternoon
- 54 Summer Quartet: Evening
- 55 Summer Quartet: Night

4
Silver-Screen

- 59 Who Is Ronald Coleman?
- 61 *Last Emperor*
- 62 L'Histoire du Cinéma
- 63 Dark Bread
- 64 *Of Mice and Men*
- 65 *Song to the Moon*
- 66 I Wish I Knew, I Wish I Knew
- 67 Diebenkorn on his *Ocean Park Series*
- 68 *Night House*

- 73 Notes
- 76 Acknowledgements
- 78 Colophon

PREFACE

Following a Thread

In her memoir *One Writer's Beginnings*, Eudora Welty offers a meditation on memory in which she follows a line—a continuous thread—*seldom in a straight line, most often spiralling*. We discover how she lived *a daring life* and how she wrote her stories.

I trace a thread of my own through my life up to this point, incomprehensible at the beginning, bunched up and tangled in places, as I chase a thought or many at once, often getting lost along the way. Looking back I see the thread filled with my obsessions, repeating themselves, full of mistakes as I advance and retreat, waylaid and languishing for long periods of time until now as I stand on the other side of my life.

I see the thread so clearly—where it has been and where it is going, sprouting into several strands flowering and expanding, unfolding into multitudes.

It's been *an inward journey*, as Eudora Welty described hers. Mine carries with it a seed unmanifest (or several of them), born of an infinite potentiality traveling out into the world.

When my creations of mind and spirit pour out of my heart, they come alive and take shape, engage and inhabit the world of myself and others. And as Welty informs us, *our separate journeys converge*.

In an act of creation and re-creation, of being and becoming, this takes place in the evolution of the line I follow—where it goes and what it does. Leaving me in astonishment and wonder, this leads me into the future, revealing itself in the seen and unseen, drawing me forward forever and always.

This book is my first collection of poems culled over many years, representing a significant part of this journey. The evolving thread of that trek continues to flourish with a variety of expressions in poetry, art, and design. This book is one such example.

—Robert Perry

1 Sheets of Linen

Sheets of Linen
After a painting by Jacob van Ruisdael
View of Haarlem with Bleaching Grounds

I
Long sheets of bleached linen dry
side by side on polders outside the city

The sun peers through the clouds
into mirrors of light reflected
from the soft green earth

The Lord Regent surveys his domain
admiring the embarrassment of riches
he claims to have created

II
In the next moment
legions of *cumulonimbus*
mount an offensive and rout the sun

Shadows fall like blankets
over every gleaming surface
as vainglorious banners yield
to dark forces set upon the land

Parades are canceled
long-faced burghers crouch
on benches commiserating
their beards bristling with defeat

III
When the sun returns
and the air is sweet again

The eye of the camera obscura
opens onto a small world

The windows of the city glinting
along the canals and the square
somber curtains disappear
replaced by teams of shimmering lace

Carillon bells in church towers
rejoice like tongues in the market stalls
they clatter and sing

In this republic morning
has only just begun

van der Helstlaan 16

The dog barks at the moon

In my attic room I hear
my nickname called
from downstairs

Children play in the summer
a sailor stands on the carpet
and cops chase the robber

In the morning
I return to the table
by a large window
the blank page
before me

Clamdigger
A sculpture by Willem de Kooning

This clamdigger rides
his bike to the edge of the sea
almost every day
humming a once forgotten tune

Een liedje over de vrouw van de zee

A man of clay who stands
like a castaway sailor
gazing into the mist and brine

Here he digs and digs
and comes
to an imperfect knowledge
on an uncertain path
which led him to
the ambiguity of his life
on this foreign shore he tried
so hard to make his own

This immigrant shown
every corner of the land
the late night betrayals
and daylight madness
the unambiguous
smiles of several women

See what you have done
You made me love you

The friendship and
jealousies of the men he met
the charm of cold water flats
and barroom chatter
the pounding
and scraping on streets
and sidewalks
the way he brought
his paintings to life

That constant reaching
into wet sand
the way he entered
and grasped
the lives of so many

Here on this spit of land
against the sky
at the dawn
of creation
again and again
an opening of a door
to the sea of
a life writ on water

In studious and frenzied repair
celebration and menace
in this new world
he takes a stand of
old world glory
and despair

Yeck, Doe, Seh, Chahar, Panj
(for Amir and Esther)

Yeck, Doe, Seh, Chahar, Panj

One, Two, Three, Four, Five

I count to five in Farsi and English
to conjure up and revisit a dream
in which Art and Mathematics
crossed paths

When Amir and I were young
and very old
students together at the University
of Revolution and Flowers

When I learned how to count to five in Farsi
and Amir began to grow his beard

No more than a five o'clock shadow
but a very compelling shadow
that darkened as the evening progressed
looking more and more red
as the evening turned into a long night
of cigarettes and coffee,
discussion and disputation

In those days, we steeped ourselves
in the wisdom of Rembrandt

A wisdom found in the light
that haunted the long beards
of ancient prophets

Amir like a prophet himself
put forth ancient principles
that govern the nature
of constellations and intersections
of time and place

One day soon the arch of the sun
will shift 180 degrees toward the earth

And when the sun collapses
into a sea of angry voices
I will command my battalion
of shadows
to cover the palace of the Shah
with flames
and turn his towers into dust

Yeck, Doe, Seh, Chahar, Panj
Yeck, Doe, Seh, Chahar, Panj

I count to five on each hand
trying in vain
to awaken from my dream

Instead I see Amir's ghost
his long beard flowing
like a red sash under a white sky

I hear Esther's soft voice
reading her poems
about hummingbirds
and persimmons

She opens a window
onto a gentle night
lets the dreams of the world
come into the house
just as the scents
of the garden enter my nostrils
and fill my thoughts with a love
that cannot be shared

A love white and bewildering
like a bright summer's glare
shining across an open book

Whatever is written there
    a quatrain of love poems
    a new constitution
    a desert lullaby
    a treatise on the language of birds
        or the fate of lost souls

it cannot be deciphered
there is only the music
of blinding light

My sad song about a love
that cannot be tended
brought to flower
or appreciated except
within a dream

This is the song I sing
long into the night

Pale Trees of January

Do not forget the train
the panes of glass
with a face in every one

The smoke in the sky

We waited for our friends to return
until they disappeared completely

The sound of children playing
stops short of explaining
how or why this happens

What do I remember?

The pale trees of January
tender the branches in snow

Return of the Prodigal Son
After a painting by Rembrandt van Rijn

Across the wild earth
I wandered
without hat or coat
without the benefit
of your knowledge
or the wisdom
of your house

I lived the gaudy life
exposed to the perils
of my conceit

I traveled high and low
in search of the many
and the few

And nothing at all
drunk with fear
I shattered the night
with my laughter

Carried the stones of hunger
in my belly and stained
the earth with the blood
of my desire

Tasted the ashes of regret
my lips burning
with righteous indignation

How could I have ever known
the pleasure of your company?

How could you have known me
lost in a maze of stars
weeping at your gate?

Shoes worn thin
feet calloused and sore
from my journey
of long abandon

Spent from hard-fought
battles unable to speak
your name

Your dogs barked
without knowing why

But your soft hands
recognized me instantly
my tender skin
and the hard dark matter
of my soul

I returned
to familiar shadows
knelt in your light
within reach
of your forgiveness

You embraced me
as your own again

The dark crimson
of your mantel
flashing red
with mercy

I kissed your cheek
and whispered in your ear

I am with you now

Law Giver

Off the mountain with new laws cradled in my arms
reach the valley by nightfall, camp around midnight
empty tents billowing like clouds
smeared across the sky, banks of fires
burning high and deep, my people steeped in trance
kneel and dance around a golden idol
like flames circling a cherished moon

I raise a scarlet hand against the glare of night
against the traffic of the people I love and guided
not ready to receive the future or forsake the past

Vanitas

Memento Mori

Before the mirror
the burden of desire
settles upon the lips

the tongue

the curve of his hands

A boy stands watch
over a city of mist

where fog modifies
light and shadow
induces sleep

Errant complacent souls
reside in rows of solemn
ornate houses

hear only the muffled shocks
of progress

reports from distant airfields

continents in flames

a child found murdered
in a shallow grave

A voice on the radio
offers absolution

but the swimmer is blind

He takes oceans of water
into his lungs

starfish and anemone
attach to his body

clouds of blood stream
toward the light

All that we are searching for
we cannot find

His automobile
left upon a nearby shore

a bright metallic shell

a hollow sun
above the sea

Vanitas

Unseen Stories

According to what
perilous night
broke
unseen stories
against the light

She embraced
each tender leaf
as if it were
her very own

She is a Child's Prayer:

Mine to keep
when I lay me
down to sleep

Mine to see
throughout the day
what dreams will be

Mine to give
for all the souls
who want to live

Luchtfietser (Daydreamer)

My secondhand bicycle is stashed away
in the back of my cousin's garage
waiting for my return

It calls to me like a trusty steed

This magical bike that wants to take me
into town again, into the countryside
and the city, turn me into a citizen of the realm

The land I admire—my teacher and my friend
who indulges me the impossible proposition
that I be considered one of them

Ride down narrow streets against the wind
watch the trains of blue & yellow pass before me
shop at Ekoplaza, wander through the heather

I've been told: autumn is what's needed
to get through the winter

Now it's spring and I'm stuck indoors
I cannot return, not for a while
I'm not sure when

The world won't let us travel
except in a daydream
cycling through the clouds

Making us into poets
drifting around the room
left to stare out the window all day
and sing through the night

After feeding the cat
I lie beside her
dreaming in the dark

I awaken to another day
and measure time
in tinctures of minutes
filling up the hours

I count the days
that accumulate into weeks,
maybe even months

A pool of longing
brimming with expectation

I try to manage like medicine
into hopeful doses to be content
in my confinement

To no avail until I learn
how to keep my yearning
in check and let my attachments
pedal away into the ether

After So Many Years

Cycling down the lanes
of my childhood
the scent of oak
reaches me from
Camino de los Arboles

Flaming pyracantha leaps out
over the fences I pass
birds fly tipsy from their red berries
circling above the trees
and houses   this way and that

The way my racing thoughts
do whatever they do
they don't change a thing
the sky is still the sky

2 If You Asked Me

If You Asked Me

If you asked me, I could write a book…
about the waxwing, how he loses his sight
when the sun appears and
grows full in the sky

How his wings melt in the heat
and he falls to earth
without a sound

Except a tiny splash
in a lonesome sea

If you asked me, I could write a book…
about how hope can fly away
in a mustard sky

How the clueless merlin
loses his magical powers
to ensnare the truth
in his claws before
it scurries away

If you asked me, I could write a book…
about the house finch who strains
his voice to serenade
his intended

How his expressed desire
to set up house falls on deaf ears

Until…before he knows it
he's sweeping the floor
and putting the kids to bed

If you asked me, I could write a book…
about the dark-eyed junco of earthbound habits
and lofty aspirations

How he pecks at the ground
and favors the safety of *terra firma*

Even though he's known to dart about
and sing in springtime

Exercising his freedom
to explore the ethereal province
of a high branch—or the open sky

River Pavilion, Mountain Colors
After a painting and colophon by Ni Zan

The sound of the rain of the second month has not stopped even in the eleventh month. The boats of the Three Rivers paddle toward Wujiang. As if drunk I cannot wake up from spring's melancholy while waves and wild winds beat against my window.

In 1368, on the tenth day of the third month, my friend Shugui invited me to visit his monkish dwelling. He asked me for a painting on this paper, so I playfully painted *River Pavilion, Mountain Colors* and inscribed a recent poem on the right.

Signed,
Zan

My window speaks fluently

across the small room

where I have taken refuge

There is no escaping

the sound of the raging river

or the colors of the mountain.

In 2003, on the last day of the fourth month,

I cannot find my hands for my face.

Moss Cove, Point Lobos

Today I linger
by a small, sheltered bay
instead of the open sea

I hear the familiar voice
of waves attending
with gracious solicitude
their presence
gentile
here in the cove

sea otters float
on their kelp beds
neither offer nor invite
speculation on the waves
that pass beneath them

fog retreats
to a respectful distance
just beyond the sea
on the hills nearby
lined with a row
of low cypress

a parade of venerables
who swallow their pride
crouch and kneel
close to the earth

I ask for no more
than this kind of beauty

the quietness of stones
ancient and content

a continent of peace
in a small place
close to the heart

Hawk Hill

Sentries stand at their posts
waiting to count the raptors
and accipiters
as if collecting and recording
the sands of time

What do they expect to gain?

Each bird brings with it
the history of the world

its wings let the thermals
lift its graceful body higher

revealing itself
to the sky as it soars

the trail of our gaze
following the sweep
of its epic cycle—

Achilles resting on air
before the battle begins

before he turns
suddenly toward his prey

and we learn
in the blink of an eye

what the blind poet Homer
meant to say and did

Great Blue Heron Takes Flight

open fields
morning fog
see what the Ohlone saw

the Great Blue Heron
nesting in burial grounds
lifts its wings

rises above
flowering mustard

into the sky
amulet against regret

makes precious what is
diminished or destroyed

what is drawn out of
the hollows of memory

to soften the hard lesson
of what is here and now
and what is gone forever

Valley of the Gaping Mouth

Branches of redbud
gave color
to the baskets used
to hold acorn mush
a staple of the Yosemite Miwok

generations of weavers
thread and coiled
thin strands of wood and reed
making them sing
in the wilderness
like the snow-melt creeks
and eternal myths
that ran through the valley
called Ah-wah'-nee
Valley of the Gaping Mouth

Black acorn paste mixed
with manzanita berries for taste

the meat of coyote
deer and black bear cooked
over a fire of cedar bark

stories were told across that fire

feeding the hungry mouths
the hungry hearts of the people
who became the rocks
and birds of this valley

The people who became the light
glancing off the polished granite above
and the tumble of boulders below

the reflection of Mirror Lake
slowly disappearing
like the yawning mouth
of contentment closing
after a long and pleasurable meal

followed by the dark forest of sleep
inhabited by a river of dreams
that have become
the legends of this valley

Early Spring

Early spring explodes
    before our eyes

a new love dresses
      for dinner

the perfume of the garden
    descends

        like a dream

hearts pounding
        at every flower

Summer Interior

morning
takes us
to the sea

after breakfast
spent in
our pajamas

Matisse
for us
all day long

summer
interior with
open window
a comfortable
armchair

me watching you
reading
at the table

bright clouds
flowers
and the sea
streaming in

our skin
bathed
in sunlight
we are free

Clarity of Autumn

Gone the gauzy
warmth
of daydream
that was summer

the clarity
of autumn
arrives

the gaunt sunlight
long-faced shadows
etched upon the saw
tooth mountain cheek

veins of regret
running through it

If Not, Winter

upon castle walls
worn down
by war

a distant flute
plays
against the sky

old bones may
learn to take
the bite

but it is
no defense
against the madness
that prevents Spring
from showing
her face

when the earth is
nothing but dust with fires
smoldering

wailing heard
over the fallen:

if not joy, Winter

[title from a fragment
of Sappho's poetry]

3 Dance of Hours

Dance of Hours

finding the center
of a long afternoon

the pitcher
—watch spring
of the game's
clockwork

winds up
into a question
mark

rises, pivots
extends to ask
what is
possible

in his delivery
and the batter's
reply   we learn

Perhaps in Spring

Perhaps in spring
a short distance from stardust
I discovered the fragrance
of tangerine blossoms—
the subject of my daydream

Sitting in sunlight
letting myself think
that I belong to
this enchanted world
and there I would remain

In this house of staircases and mirrors
a mural of watery Venice floating above
the furniture and large red cushions
strewn about the hearth
where a body could drift
for hours leafing quietly
through the morning papers

And find oneself in a state of bliss
listening to the music
of water lapping
against ancient stones
of buildings with golden spires

I have wondered since, if I could return
to this Garden of Earthly Delights

Perhaps in spring, I think
as the song of my daydream lingers
I should never think of spring
for that would surely break
my heart in two

Before the Revolution

The tallest redwood in the neighborhood
and the best climbing tree stood
in the Bridgeman backyard.

As a boy I reached its highest branches
and perched there for hours
watching the parade of grown ups
gather on the patio for Saturday
afternoon cocktails.

The new generation assembled
attempting to enjoy the best years
of their lives... *walking across the lawn
with drink in hand and lust in their pants...*
treating the future as a foregone conclusion.

Mrs. Bridgeman sat on her chaise
Helen of Troy of the cocktail hour
lounging in the middle of her entourage.

Turning the ice in her drink slowly
with one finger extended across
the frigid contents of her glass
as if the the entire gathering
revolved around her.

Leisurely sipping her Scotch and soda
Mrs. Bridgeman was a nest of secrets.

Beneath a glacier of self-assurance
there grew a fissure, a desperate seeking
an urgent fire in the darkness reaching
the surface where she pursued
her voiceless ambitions in a voiceless room
before the revolution began.

Barefoot Boy

the barefoot boy
face full of freckles
could not be the same
person who lost his life
the minute his foot
hit the accelerator pedal

the town mourned his passing
but you can bet
that somewhere in the night
someone breathes
a sigh of relief

Good Government

Good government is
the way my grandfather sat
on the couch

Doing the crossword puzzle
in pen from start to finish

He took a walk after dinner
every day of his life

A man of practical means
while I sat freezing
far from home
in an Arizona desert
trying to stay warm
with a pair of socks
pulled over my hands

Watching the Homol'ovi sun retire
and the Homol'ovi moon rise
in the open sky

Me without fear—or gloves

Place of Peace (Shiloh)

In this place of peace
our angel weeps

a tiny creek
surrounded by a sea
of regiments

the machines of war
wait for glory

in rain and darkness
blinding light
the vacant trees of
dawn find them
unawares

the republic
not the least
bit whole

From the *Civil War Suite*

Messenger of Love

Hold him oh Savior!
In thine arms
and let him henceforth
be a messenger of love
betwixt our human hearts
and Thee

He will speak to us
in our prayers
have us understand
man shall slay his brother

the chestnut sky
shall further the cause
of simple truths
impossible to attain

the message less clear
now than it ever was
in each war
armaments exceed
the strategy
fear and death are chosen
over peace and love

in conversation and song
he will regale us
with public rejoicing
and private sorrow

the voice of drums
echoing in our hearts
exceeds the tranquility
of the grass around his feet

we ask him what
hope is this glory

The Dead at Antietam

Many fell at Antietam
their blood flowed
onto the land
not long before the
Emancipation Proclamation
—enacted January 1863

the cause of freedom
thought to ennoble
the carnage and
promote victory

images of the battle
captured on glass
negatives made
into positives
infused with light
printed on paper and
exhibited to the public

the eyes of the world
looked upon them
matched the lists of names
and dispositions read
to the horrors revealed
in those photographs

From the *Civil War Suite*

the search for truth
and reason pursued
as history records
each furrow
torn across the page
like seeds planted
in a shallow
unsettled earth

below an empty sky
crops sown
with shouts and wails
consumed by fire

flames glow white
conjure images of young men
twisted and spent
possessed by demons
it would seem

this passion play
all about shadows and light
dreams of home

against all hope
these boys will get there
one way or another

forever free indeed

Soldier in the Night

The healing hand rests upon my brow.
His fingers stained by my tears.

The war is over, but I am not home yet.
My bed is cold, the sheets are clean.

My solemn oath still in effect.
I have not spoken for days.

The doctor asks me to walk across the room.
The pages of my book turn slowly.

I make my way at my own pace.
There is no other choice but to try.

The soldier in the night
haunts me at every turn.

Smoke rises above his head
surrounds him like a halo.

I am blessed to be alive
while so many have perished.

I can't begin to tell you.
The soldier in the night remains.

Copper and Wood
from an exhibit of Roi Partridge
and Richard Wagener

In this exhibit a correspondence
between two artists ensues
who etched and printed plates
one on copper, the other on wood

Sheets of paper sent through the press
produce the printed page where we find
> ink flooding the retina
> with mountains and trees
> stones and sky

in the hush one recalls
the poet Emily Dickenson:
> *There's a certain slant of light*
> *when the landscape listens*
> *shadows hold their breath*

Summer Quartet

Morning

Light arrives early
already dressed for the day
the temperature of green
—a quiet beginning
the spell of dreams
slowly lifting

The shape of promises
made the day before returns
the weight of them remains
as new thoughts appear
among the leaves of the trees

Sunlight declares itself
in no uncertain terms
there is no choice but to watch
and listen to what comes next

The heat and glare present
themselves in whatever transpires
throughout the day
until it takes a long breath
and fades into the dark of night
with the promise of stars
and more dreams followed by
a new morning

Afternoon

Summer also brings regret
in the heat and glare
of long afternoons
blinding me to the gift
of the here and now

Training me instead
into an airy dream
of my youth—
that other country
where I languish
in what was
and might have been

Drifting among faint clouds
I shape into apparitions
of flesh and blood events
storylines I wish
had played out and didn't

Without a hint
of an honest regret
I carry with me
that impossible wish
my summers could
repeat themselves and
give me a second chance

Evening

The day takes
a long breath
fading into night
I wander through a sunset
garden spread across the sky
into the air of darkness
growing around me

The glare now gone, the heat remains
pressing me into a steady stream
of thoughts—my inner voice speaking
accompanied by a symphony
of crickets and cicadas singing

In a vast universe drawing near
into a comfortable embrace
I feel my freedom
expand and flourish
on this summer evening
giving itself over
to a promise of stars
and whatever dreams
emerge when I sleep

Night

I sink into the heat
of a noisy darkness
wrestle with my sheets
wishing I could swim
smoothly off to sleep

Eventually I drift into
a dream as vivid
as any midrash and
equally instructive

I swim in a pool
of silence after a storm
Elijah the lifeguard
lurking there
behind his shades
zinc oxide down his nose

I float on my back
looking up into
a cloudless sky
a portrait of Infinity
—never have I known
such bliss as this

I wake up to the heat
unable to go back
to sleep when I greet
my misgivings
I catalogue each one
until morning

This is when I long
for the dawn to wash
them away and replace them
with my most vaulted aspirations

The ceilings I wish to paint
depicting the realms of heaven
with an infinite exquisite sun
shining beyond the clouds
that seek to obscure them

Or the statues I'd like to sculpt
chipping away at the stone
to reveal the very substance
that enables the human spirit
to flourish and endure

From these summer nights
I pull myself out of bed
praise the morning light
ready to discover what
the day will bring

4 Silver-Screen

Who is Ronald Coleman?

The difference between the known
and the unknown

The difference between the voice
unspoken and the voice

Spoken for the first time
emerging from the mist

The wash of light and shadow

From the pantomime
of comedy and tragedy

From the hill cliffs of the silver-screen
across the heath or on a busy sidewalk

From the cloud of some nightclub
dispensing advice over a cocktail

Or wisdom on the gallows
nodding to the Fates

Standing before our hero
like midnight satin and silk
as thin as his moustache

Cut by his wry smile
and an almost imperceptible wince
felt under his brow

The tale of two cities
in a long career of measured steps
out of the gloom into the light

Of whatever the eyes will say on cue

Of whatever way the words will grow
into forests and stars

Our civilization from in front of
the camera and the microphone

The difference between the known
and the unknown

All for the price of admission

The Last Emperor

I am Aisin Gioro Pu Yi
the last emperor of China
Lord of Ten Thousand Years

I am the cricket
in the Great Hall
of the Forbidden City

I am a truly useful person
after all

I am a gardener
with a purpose in life

I am the fisherman's song
for violin and piano

I am the father of disgrace
and the appreciative son
of kindness and virtue

I am a butterfly and a traitor
imprisoned without love

I am a singer in Tienjin
singing *Am I Blue?*

I am a careless tennis player
ready to plead guilty or innocent

I am a reader of fire in the night
rousted from my bed but not sleep

I am the bicycle riding
on the rooftops of heaven

L'Histoire du Cinéma

Grace Kelly like a dream
hovers in Crêpe de Chine

her shadow falling over
a slumbering Jimmy Stewart

bathed in silvery light
next to an open window

descending she
awakens him with
a slow and precious kiss

Dark Bread

We taste the dark bread
of his brooding silhouette

Scale the heft of his brow
in medium close up
conversant
with his dark eyes
and acrobatic charm

Yet the more we look
the less we know
the more we see of him
of what he shows us on screen

the more amazed we are
at how he secures and
promotes our sense
of well being

How satisfied we are
with the mystery of him

the elusive, fleeting
candlelit supper of him
which we partake and dream of
when our hunger returns

Of Mice and Men

Our hero walks the Long Valley
with his bindlestiff grin

along with his gentle-hearted companion
of unintended consequences

through a landscape of *promised joy*
a soft wind sending them forth
to apply their kindness

through fields and fields of wheat
in a world of dirt
and fences and cruelty
that can never be changed

our ever hopeful hero does
what he can
what must be done
even when right is wrong

learning a barn and boxcar lesson
that it is a narrow stream
finding its way into a wider river
running *deep and green*

Song to the Moon

My love is waiting for me
dreaming in your silvery light

I cannot stay, much as I wish to
for I must return to the sea
where I can breathe again

Kiss her once for me
and tell her why I must leave

I'm bound to a world she cannot touch
a river of tears that has grown
into an ocean of peril and darkness
a fate I must fight far from your light

Embrace my darling love for me
as she sleeps and when she awakens
to her world without me

May she remember, as I will
the shore where we met
the swollen blossoms
glittering leaves and
the promising earth of
what our love could have been
what I long for so dearly

Let not this dream fade
from her heart

May she think of me fondly
as your light begins to disappear

May she greet the full face
of morning and all her days
without regret

I Wish I Knew, I Wish I Knew

Hear those cries from the wilderness of my being
Manifestos against the enemies of imagination

Trying to bring order out of chaos
I line up my blocks from end to end

Leap from one moment
and climb into the rocket ship of the next

No time to notice how the universe reacts
To the touch of my hand

I listen to the heartbeat of my tongue
the way I trace the map of unconditional love

For the kingdom of the body has many mansions

For those like me who don't know how
to love in a one-note world

Hear those cries from the wilderness of my being
Manifestos against the enemies of imagination

For I am the train of countless reflections
Arriving and departing

Where am I going?

I wish I knew, I wish I knew, I wish I knew

Diebenkorn on his *Ocean Park Series*

In these paintings, I translate them
from the French—interiors with
a view of the world
seen through an open window.

Outside is inside:
This is what happens
when you have a studio
a short distance from the ocean.

I'd walk there, but I paint it instead.

In the afternoon, I leave to teach a class;
when I return, the paint is still wet.

I change things again.

There is no other way
when you have so many choices.

I try several things
until it works, until I'm content.

If not, I go to another painting
and see what happens.

Everything is perfect
or nothing is.

Night House

in the night house
with two windows
burning

what will I say
to the cabinet of
high expectations
not to mention
the anxious chest
of drawers

I wander
from room to room
and send my love
to the candlestick
standing on top
of the bookcase
behind the sofa

a pair of slippers
belongs to the carpet
just as I belong
to this house

I stumble about
knock your hatbox
off the dresser
in the bedroom

while the dog
wonders where
I'm going to sleep
tonight

be still my heart
the toothbrush sits
in its holder just so

the pale blue wallpaper
the color of songs
of Arcadian pleasure
luxe, calme et volupté

my pajamas
the color of
a winter's dawn
before the moon
has had a chance
to escape

before I have
a chance to
seal my fate
in the kitchen
the refrigerator
purring before me

the knives in their
drawers unwilling
to divulge their
secrets

they won't even tell
the fingers that
hold them what
they already know

the cat jumps
up gingerly just
as I had once
tread cautiously
during the war
of attrition

when it was all
I could do
not to cry over
spilled milk

what did I imagine
you'd say when
I climbed the stairs
the last time we danced
the two-step

you in your
crimson dressing
gown standing up
to sing each chorus

I wish I could sing
like the engineer
when he told us about
the last steam train
in America

winding its way home
somewhere down South
crossing a river bridge
blowing its whistle by
a drive-in movie theater

when is the last time
you played Kick the Can
and lost your shoe
to the sky

the wallpaper gone
mute like the window
shade with summer
nearly gone

the heat finally
easing up
cool air drifting
into the house
without a sound

before we stop trying
and close our eyes
we reach for
the empty suitcase
in the closet

a suitcase we'll fill up
with dreams for a trip
down the garden path
and why not

tomorrow is skulking
out there in the dark
just beyond
the porch light
waiting to tell us
where to go
and what to do

full of promises
and a fist full of flowers
too good to be true
too good to pass up

we are like the night
lovers ever hopeful
longing for daylight
singing in a shower
of stars waiting
for dawn

*Someday if all my prayers
are answered*

*I'll hear a footstep
on the stair*

*with an anxious heart
I'll hurry to the door and
maybe you'll be there*

NOTES

Half Title – An excerpt from an article by Piet Mondriaan in "Natural- and Abstract Reality" in *De Stijl Magazine*, August 1919, Vol. 2, No. 10, page 112.

Preface – *One's Writer's Beginnings* by Eudora Welty. Cambridge, Massachusetts: Harvard University Press 1984; Delivered as three lectures at Harvard University in April 1983.

Chapter 1 Heading – Title of the poem "Sheets of Linen" thst was inspired by the oil painting *View of Haarlem with Bleaching Ground*, c1665, by Jacob van Ruisdael, a detail reproduced here with permission from the Mauritshuis, The Hague, The Netherlands.

"Clamdigger" (page 6) – Poem about the life and career of Dutch born American artist Willem de Kooning with the title from his sculpture of that name, modeled in clay in 1972, cast in bronze in 1976, located in the Hirshorn Museum and Sculpture Garden, Washington, D.C. "*Een liedje over de vrouw van de zee*" in English is "the song about the woman from the sea."

"*Return of the Prodigal Son*" (pages 12-14) – Poem inspired by the oil painting of that name by Rembrandt van Rijn, c1661-1669, located in the Hermitage Museum, St. Petersburg, Russia.

"Law Giver" (page 13) – Poem inspired by a tapestry of Moses at Chapel of the Holy Cross, Sedona, Arizona (artist unknown).

"Luchtfietser (Daydreamer)" (page 14) – Poem about my experience during the recent pandemic, appearing originally on coronagedicht.nl in 2020, and published later in the collection *Mijn overbuurvrouw is een meeuw*, Uitgeverij Liverse, 2021.

Chapter 2 Heading – Title of the poem "If You Asked Me" (page 25-26) riffs on the song lyric "If you asked me, I could write a book…" written by Lorenz Hart with music by Richard Rogers for "If I Could Write a Book," in the 1940 musical *Pal Joey*. The drawing of a dark-eyed junco is by Robert Perry.

"***River Pavilion, Mountain Colors***" (page 27) – The poem responds to the artist's colofon contained in the ink painting of this title by the Yuan dynasty literati painter Ni Zan, located in the Asian Art Museum, San Francisco, California.

"***If Not, Winter***" (page 37) – The poem title is a fragment of poetry by Sappho that is the title of a volume of her poetry translated by Anne Carson, reprinted with permission from Vintage Books, division of Random House, Inc., New York, New York, August 2003. The body of the poem is inspired and informed by the Japanese film *Ran* (Chaos) by Akira Kurosawa, his brilliant adaptation of Shakespeare's "King Lear."

Chapter 3 Heading – The image accompanied by the poem title "Dance of Hours" (page 41) about baseball is a detail of a photograph of Yankee Stadium reproduced from the slipcase of *Baseball Encyclopedia*, Macmillan, 1969.

"***Perhaps in Spring***" (page 42) – The poem title is excerpted from the song "I Get Along Without You Very Well" sung by Diana Krall in my memory, lyrics and music composed by Hoagy Carmichael in 1939.

"**Before the Revolution**" (page 43) – The excerpt "…*walking across the lawn with drink in hand and lust in their pants*…" was drawn from my memory of a passage in a John Cheever story for The New Yorker magazine editor William Shawn excised as being salacious.

"**Good Government**" (page 45) – *Homol'ovi* is the name of an ancient people who lived in north central Arizona near Winslow.

Civil War Suite (pages 46-50) – A selection of poems from this suite: "Place of Peace (Shiloh)" "Messenger of Love" "The Dead at Antietum" contained in an artist book inspired by the documentary series *The Civil War* by Ken Burns produced by Public Broadcasting Corporation in 1990.

The "Messenger of Love" inscription is found on the *Angel of Grief* grave monument of Henry Clay Lathrop, brother of Jane Lathrop Stanford, located in the Arboretum, Stanford University. The text in italics in the poem "The Dead at Antietam" are words in the Emancipation Proclaimation.

"*Copper and Wood*" (page 51) – This poem was prompted by an exhibit at the Mills College Art Museum of that name featuring the prints of Roi Partrigde from copper plates and Richard Wagener from wood blocks.

The Emily Dickinson poem, number 320 (in the public domain), appeared in the exhibit brochure by Jan Elsted (Barbarian Press) that she excerpted from a review "California in Relief" published in *Parenthesis Magazine* (Fine Press Book Association), Autumn 2010.

Chapter 4 Heading – The image with the title "Silver-Screen" is a photograph (in public domain) of Ronald Colman and Vilma Banky in the silent film *The Winning of Barbara Worth* released in 1926.

"*Last Emperor*" (page 61) – inspired by the film of that name directed by Bernardo Bertolucci, released by Columbia Pictures, 1987.

"**L'Histoire du Cinèma**" (page 62) – Inspired by Alfred Hiitchcock's *Rear Window*, Paramount Pictures, released 1954.

"*Of Mice and Men*" (page 64) – This poem is inspired by the John Steinbeck play and movie of that name. Text in italics are words from the Robert Burns poem, "To a Mouse" from which Steinbeck drew the title of his work.

"*Song to the Moon*" (page 65) – The poem is informed by the aria of that name in the 1900 opera *Rusalka* by Antonín Dvořák.

"**Diebenkorn on his *Ocean Park Series***" (page 67) – The poem responds to a series of paintings by Richard Diebenkorn produced in his studio in Santa Monica, California, 1966-1988.

"*Night House*" (page 68) – The poem is inspired by an artist book of that name by Jody Alexander, which led to our collaboration on another kind of artist book in 2009—three cubes combining nine photos from the original work and nine stanzas of the poem selected by Alexander (See dutchpoetpress.com/artist-books).

Text in italics at the end of the poem are excerpted from the song lyrics of "Maybe You'll Be There" composed and written by Rube Bloom and Sam Gallop in 1946, as sung by Diana Krall in the version I remember.

ACKNOWLEDGEMENTS

With appreciation to those who provided crucial contributions of their knowledge and wisdom, help and support that made the publication of this book possible in a variety of ways:

Ron Guzman and Gordon Holler for giving me an extraordinary introduction to the world of art and art history.

My cousin Elsie Franken-Holt and her family for introducing me to The Netherlands.

The poetry groups Waverley Writers, Tuesdy Poets, and Saturday Poets, as welll as two poets in particular, Esther Kamkar and Charlotte Muse for providing invaluable editorial advice on the manuscript.

Printer and designer Mike Day for his keen eye and expertise.

My beloved Jessie for her understanding and encouragement over these many years, and for proofreading this book and many others.

My hearfelt thanks to everyone and everything that served as inspiration and became an essential part of my poetry and this project..

◆ ◆ ◆

These poems appeared in *Sand Hill Review* in 2005: "Clamdigger" "Yeck, Doe, Seh, Chahar, Panj" "Perhaps in Spring" and in Summer 2015: "Before the Revolution" "After So Many Years" "Dance of Hours" "Echolalia" (changed here to "I Wish I Knew, I Wish I Knew") "Pale Trees of January" "Silver-Screen" (changed here to "Who is Ronald Coleman?").

"Luchtfietser (Daydreamer)" appeared in coronagedicht.nl in 2019, portside.org in 2020, and the collection *Mijn achterbuurvrouw is een meeuw*, Uitgeverij Liverse, Dordrecht, The Netherlands, 2021.

COLOPHON

Display and Text Face: Adobe Caslon Pro—the digital version designed by Carol Twomley for Adobe in 1989 based on the old style typeface from Great Britian designed by William Caslon in London, first released in 1722.

Book Design by Robert Perry, author and founder of Dutch Poet Press, Palo Alto, California.

Printing by IngramSpark of the Ingram Content Group, LaVergne, Tennessee.

www.ingramcontent.com/pod-product-compliance
Lightning Source LLC
Chambersburg PA
CBHW061739070526
44585CB00024B/2745